Sylvia Hadjetian

Mary Shelley's Frankenstein and Feminism

GRIN Verlag

Bibliografische Information der Deutschen Nationalbibliothek:

Die Deutsche Bibliothek verzeichnet diese Publikation in der Deutschen National-
bibliografie; detaillierte bibliografische Daten sind im Internet über http://dnb.d-
nb.de/ abrufbar.

Imprint:

Copyright © 2001 GRIN Verlag GmbH
Druck und Bindung: Books on Demand GmbH, Norderstedt Germany
ISBN: 978-3-638-93194-6

This book at GRIN:

http://www.grin.com/en/e-book/42827/mary-shelley-s-frankenstein-and-feminism

Royal Holloway University of London   Sylvia Hadjetian

Women, Writing and Feminism

Mary Shelley's *Frankenstein*

and

Feminist Reading

Table of Contents

1. Introduction

Mary W. Shelley wrote her novel *Frankenstein* in a time in which women were expected to stay at home, care fore the children and do the household. Men normally worked outside the home in the public sphere, the division of roles was very strict[1] and men were valued over women[2].

Science and research were domains exclusively for men. Although she was no scientist, her husband and several other scientists, e.g. Erasmus Darwin, influenced Mary Shelley. She has however somehow entered a male sphere, which was normally forbidden for her.

This could perhaps be one of the reasons why she did not publish her novel herself but her husband Percy.

Another reason for this could be that women writer had a bad reputation. Their works were normally regarded as bad because they did not have a good education[3]. A woman writer was regarded as "unladylike"[4], she was expected to be "modest, chaste and docile"[5] and an "angel"[6]. The only duty of a woman was to be a good wife and especially a good mother, she was normally the only responsible for the education of the children because the men went to work and never participated in nurture.

This essay will examine the role of each woman in *Frankenstein* in the 19th century, the importance of a mother for a child and the failure of Victor Frankenstein to create and nurture a child without a woman.

---

[1] Cf. Anne Kostelanetz Mellor, *Mary Shelley: Her Life, Her Fiction, Her Monsters* (New York & London: Routledge, 1988), p. 115.
[2] Cf. Ibid.
[3] Cf. Johanna M. Smith, "'Cooped Up with 'Sad Trash': Domesticity and the Sciences in *Frankenstein*", in *Frankenstein: Complete Authoritative Text with Biographical, Historical and Cultural Contexts, Critical History and Essays from Contemporary Critical Perspectives*, ed. Johanna M. Smith (New York: St. Martin's, 2000) pp. 315-316.
[4] Fred Botting, *Making Monstrous: Frankenstein, Criticism, Theory* (Manchester: Manchester UP, 1991), p. 108.
[5] Ibid.
[6] Ibid.

2. The role of women in *Frankenstein*

2.1. Margaret Saville

The first woman the reader gets to know in *Frankenstein* is Margaret Saville, the sister of Robert Walton. Margaret and Robert write letters to each other while Robert is on his way to the North Pole. His sister stays at home, which is typical for those times. The women were supposed to be at home, occupied with the household and nurture of the children while the men went to work. In Robert's case, he is a "real" man risking dangers on his way to his aim. In his letters, he tells his sister about his thoughts, sorrows and adventures and the story about Frankenstein and his monster. He needs her letters; they support him in hard times ("I need them most to support my spirits"[7]) and in one of those letters, he thanks her for her "love and kindness"[8] and her "gentle and feminine fosterage"[9]. So he is probably Margaret's younger brother and as his elder sister, it is her duty to care for him and to take part in his education. In the 19th century, women were expected to help in the household and to look after their younger brothers and sisters. They have a mother role, like Margaret who worries about her brother and who tries to encourage him whenever she can.

2.2. Caroline Beaufort

Caroline Beaufort is the next woman introduced in the novel. She is the daughter of a merchant who is the best friends of Alphonse Frankenstein. After her father has lost a lot of money, Caroline starts working in order to earn money to survive. There is no mother and when her father becomes ill, she cares for him until his death, being the perfect daughter. His death makes her "an orphan and a beggar"[10]. Alphones Frankenstein, "a protecting spirit"[11], rescues her and marries her two years later. She is an "ideal of female devotion"[12], at first, she is devoted to her ill and poor father, then she marries his best friend and is devoted to him[13]. But Alphonse treats her as an equal; he is thankful, does everything for her and wants to recompense her "for the

---

[7] Mary Shelley, *Frankenstein*, Three Gothic Novels, ed. Peter Fairclough (London: Penguin Books, 1986), p. 276.
[8] Ibid., p. 272.
[9] Ibid., p. 274.
[10] Ibid., p. 290.
[11] Ibid.
[12] Mellor, *Mary Shelley*, p. 116.
[13] Cf. Ibid.

sorrows she had endured"[14]. He stops working after their marriage in order to be able to travel a lot with his wife for whom the climate changes are good because of her ill health. When their first son Victor is born, he helps her with his nurture, which is quite untypical for a man in those times. Caroline is "the perfect daughter, wife and mother"[15]. There is also a kind of indebtedness[16] in her actions. Alphonse has rescued her and now she has to fulfil certain duties for him. She is a good wife, housewife and childcare provider[17]. Also as part of her indebtedness, she visits the poor in order to help them like a "guardian angel"[18]. On one of her visits, she finds Elizabeth whom she takes with her.

2.3. Elizabeth Lavenza

Elizabeth Lavenza is the motherless daughter of a Milanese nobleman who has disappeared after having given her into a poor foster family. Her mother has died when Elizabeth was born. Alphonse allows Caroline to keep her, which shows that Caroline cannot take decisions on her own. Elizabeth is like a gift for little Victor, he regards her as his possession, she is "more than sister"[19] for him and they call each other cousins. She is very beautiful, a "living spirit of love"[20] and the two children have a happy childhood together. When Elizabeth gets scarlet fever, Caroline is again the ideal of self-sacrifice[21]. She cares for Elizabeth, not worrying about her own health. But her role as Elizabeth's nurse kills Caroline. She dies a few days later. This care is typical for a loving mother. Just before her death, she tells Elizabeth to take her place in the family. Elizabeth takes this role immediately, she becomes the new "mother", comforting everybody after Caroline's death, forgetting her own sadness. She is also indebted to the family because Alphonse saved her life by allowing Caroline to keep her. When Victor goes to university in Ingolstadt, it is her who writes letters to him, also when he is on his journey to Scotland. She always worries about him like a mother and in her letters, her main topic is her family, typical for a woman of this time because she had nothing else in her life besides her home. It is

---

[14] Shelley, *Frankenstein*, p. 291.
[15] Botting, *Making monstrous*, p. 100.
[16] Cf. Smith, "Cooped Up", p. 312.
[17] Cf. Mellor, *Mary Shelley*, p. 116.
[18] Shelley, *Frankenstein*, p. 292.
[19] Ibid., p. 293.
[20] Ibid., p. 297.
[21] Cf. Mellor, *Mary Shelley*, p. 116.

also her who asks Clerval to accompany Victor to Scotland. Also typical is that she stays at home waiting for her Victor while he is away in order to study and fulfil his dreams. After the death of William, Elizabeth thinks that his death is her fault because she has given William the miniature the murderer wanted to have. It should have been her duty to protect him as a good mother but she has failed although it was not really her fault. As a good daughter, she also wants to keep her promise to marry Victor. In one of her letters, she asks him if he still wants to marry her and he says yes. She is happy and looks forward to their wedding although Victor has a secret. But as a very good friend, she knows how to comfort him[22]. In her wedding night, she feels that something terrible will happen but as a devoted wife, she does what her husband Victor tells her and goes to bed alone where the monster kills her. She dies in appreciation of her obedience.

2.4. Justine Moritz

Another typical fate has Justine Moritz. Caroline Beaufort also saves her from her mother who treats her badly. She can start working as a servant of the family. She adores her new family and tries to imitate them, especially Caroline. When her mother is ill, she cares for her although she has never received love from her but it is her duty as a good daughter. When she is accused of having murdered William, she believes that God will help her because he knows that she is not guilty ("rely on the justice of [...] laws"[23]). At her trial, she is very calm and has almost given up hope because she knows that there is no solution for her. Although Elizabeth tries to defend her innocence, Justine is condemned. she lies confessing her guilt because she is afraid of the hell fire and wants to obtain absolution[24]. She is forced to lie. If she had not been just a servant, the judges would have been forced to free her or at least to check her guilt once more. But the judges have no pity on her. Justine has also indebtedness for the Frankensteins who saved her from her mother[25]. Justine is like a mother for William and takes part in the search for him ("maternal search for William"[26]). She has also no mother because her mother does not love her and she is said to have

---

[22] Shelley, *Frankenstein*, p. 461.
[23] Ibid., p. 343.
[24] Ibid., p. 350.
[25] Cf. Smith, "Cooped Up", p. 321-322.
[26] Ibid., p. 322.

caused her mother's death[27]. So she is said to be responsible for her mother's and little William's death. Her name alludes to "justice" but her trial is a symbol of " the injustice treatment of the women"[28] at that time; she shows no protest because she has no alternatives.

2.5. Agatha De Lacey

Agatha De Lacey, the sister of Felix De Lacey, works also at home while her brother works outside. Most of the time, she is occupied with the household but sometimes, Felix and Agatha help each other and work together ("The young man was constantly employed out of doors, and the girl in various laborious occupations within"[29]). Both of them care for their blind father, not only the daughter, which is uncommon. There is also no mother in this family.

2.6. Safie

Safie, whose name means "wisdom"[30], is Felix's love and the most modern woman of those represented in *Frankenstein*. She should become his wife because Felix helped her father to escape from prison. But they both fall in love anyway. When he is free, her father is against their marriage and Safie decides to run away from her father in search for Felix. Safie has had a very liberal education; her mother was a slave who told her to reach independence ("to aspire to higher powers of intellect and an independence of spirit forbidden to the female followers of Muhammad"[31]). Safie risks her life and leaves her family for Felix, she leaves her home and travels on her own. She is "an instance of female resistance"[32] and a symbol of "women's capacity for activity and autonomy"[33], her courage is rewarded with Felix's love.

---

[27] Cf. Margaret Homans, "Bearing Demons: Frankenstein's Circumvention of the Maternal", in *Mary Shelley's Frankenstein: Critical Essays*, ed. Harold Bloom (New York: Chelsea House, 1987), p. 134.
[28] Botting, *Making Monstrous*, p. 101.
[29] Shelley, *Frankenstein*, p. 375.
[30] U. C. Knoepflmacher, "Thoughts on the Aggression of Daughters", in *The Endurance of Frankenstein: Essays on Mary Shelley's Novel*, eds. George Levine and U. C. Knoepflmacher (Berkeley & London: California UP, 1979), p. 98.
[31] Shelley, *Frankenstein*, p. 390.
[32] Botting, *Making Monstrous*, p. 101.
[33] Ibid.

3. The importance of a mother for a child

3.1. The development of the monster

Frankenstein shows clearly the importance of a mother for the nurture of a child. Victor fails completely in his role as a father. He chooses body parts for his child which do not fit together, a loving mother would never do this. He only seems to have his "wonder" in mind, he is careless and selfish, does not even think of a mother. He has placed obstacles in his child's path and influenced its life in a negative way. A mother would do only the best for her child. After the birth, he describes his child as a "catastrophe"[34]; he is shocked and runs away instead of reaching out to the newborn. He is afraid of his own child, which is very abnormal for a parent. The monster wants to get in contact with its father but Victor has no sense of responsibility or fatherhood and therefore, the monster stays alone. It makes its first experiences on its own and learns how to survive without the help of a parent. The De Laceys become a kind of foster family for the monster, it learns how to speak etc. and about society. But nobody loves it, so it gets aggressive and looks for its creator. Victor promises to create a female monster but he does not keep his promise. The monster has turned into a murderer because of vengeance, rejection and frustration. In the end, it loses also its father. This development of the monster shows how important the role of a mother is in the education of a child. Victor's attempt to create a human being without a woman and to nurture it fails completely. He is so shocked after the birth that he rejects it and is never able to love it. Instead of caring for his child, he is occupied with his own interests, he is not able to combine work and nurture, and he has no feeling of responsibility. Every mother would have been expected to love and care for her child, not caring about its appearance etc.

3.2. Childbirth

Victor tries to take the normal role of getting children away from women[35]. Childbirth is the "female's primary biological function and source of cultural power"[36]. He does

---

[34] Shelley, *Frankenstein*, p. 318.
[35] Cf. Botting, *Making Monstrous*, p. 101.
[36] Mellor, *Mary Shelley*, p. 115.

not really want to get a child; he wants to get power over nature and women because childbirth is more or less the only thing where men depend on women[37].

Mary Shelley was herself a mother. This novel is often seen as a "birth myth"[38]. Her own mother died at Mary's birth and the topic of the novel can be interpreted as "a woman writer's anxieties about bearing children"[39] and what happens if the child has no loving and caring mother or if the nurture of the parents fails completely.

4. Conclusion

Women play a marginal role in *Frankenstein*, there are only few mothers in the plot and all of them die soon. The women in the novel are always, despite Safie, represented as passive and the men are active ("feminine passivity and masculine activity"[40]). Women are regarded as "devoted, selfless, loving, and passive"[41] and fulfil their duties with "hardly a complaint"[42]. They seem to be "possessable"[43], "interchangeable within the domestic circle"[44] and "function [...] as signs of and conduits for men's relations with other men"[45]. Johnson describes them as "beautiful, selfless, boring nurturers and victims who never experience inner conflict or true desire"[46], independent women did not exist in those times[47], women like Safie were an exception.

But the negative development of the monster shows the importance of such a loving mother for the nurture of a child. Women shall never be so passive and let men like Victor take them away their most important role of childbirth. But Mary Shelley's monster and Victor's failure show very well how important the role of women as mothers really is and always will be.

---

[37] Cf. Smith, "Cooped Up", p. 330.
[38] Ibid., p. 103.
[39] Homans, *Bearing Demons*, p. 145.
[40] Smith, "Cooped Up", p. 318.
[41] Botting, *Making Monstrous*, p. 100.
[42] Ibid.
[43] Mellor, *Mary Shelley*, p. 115.
[44] Smith, "Cooped Up", pp. 322-323.
[45] Ibid., p. 323.
[46] Barbara Johnson, "My Monster/My Self", in *Mary Shelley's Frankenstein: Critical Essays*, ed. Harold Bloom (New York: Chelsea House, 1987), p. 55.
[47] Cf. Mellor, *Mary Shelley*, p. 118.

Bibliography

Primary literature

1. Shelley, Mary, *Frankenstein*, Three Gothic Novels, ed. Peter Fairclough (London: Penguin Books, 1986), pp. 258-497.
2.

Secondary literature

1. Botting, Fred, *Making Monstrous: Frankenstein, Criticism, Theory* (Manchester: Manchester UP, 1991).
2. Homans, Margaret, "Bearing Demons: Frankenstein's Circumvention of the Maternal", in *Mary Shelley's Frankenstein: Critical Essays*, ed. Harold Bloom (New York: Chelsea House, 1987), pp. 133-153.
3. Johnson, Barbara, "My Monster/My Self", in *Mary Shelley's Frankenstein: Critical Essays*, ed. Harold Bloom (New York: Chelsea House, 1987), pp. 55-66.
4. Knoepflmacher, U. C., "Thoughts on the Aggression of Daughters", in *The Endurance of Frankenstein: Essays on Mary Shelley's Novel*, eds. George Levine and U. C. Knoepflmacher (Berkeley & London: California UP, 1979), pp. 88-119.
5. Mellor, Anne Kostelanetz, *Mary Shelley: Her Life, Her Fiction, Her Monsters* (New York & London: Routledge, 1988).
6. Smith, Johanna M., "'Cooped Up with 'Sad Trash': Domesticity and the Sciences in *Frankenstein*", in *Frankenstein: Complete Authoritative Text with Biographical, Historical and Cultural Contexts,* Critical *History and Essays from Contemporary Critical Perspectives*, ed. Johanna M. Smith (New York: St. Martin's, 2000), pp. 313-333.